CHOCOLATE WORK

TOM PHILLIPS

MEREHURST

I dedicate this book to all the chocoholics in the world

First published in 1996 by Merehurst Limited, Ferry House, 51 – 57 Lacy Road, Putney, London SW15 1PR

ISBN 1-85391-572-6

Edited by Donna Wood
Designed by Jo Tapper
Photography by Graham Tann
Colour separation by Pixel Tech. Pte Ltd, Singapore
Printed by Wing King Tong, Hong Kong

Acknowledgements
The author and publisher would like to thank the following for their assistance:
Anniversary House (Cake Decorations) Ltd., Unit 16, Elliott Road, West Howe Industrial Estate, Bournemouth, BH11 8LZ, Tel: 01202 590222;
Cake Art Ltd., Venture Way, Crown Estate, Priorswood, Taunton, TA2 8DE, Tel: 01823 321532;
Guy, Paul & Co. Ltd., Unit B4, Foundary Way, Little End Road, Eaton Socon, Cambridge PE19 3JH, Tel: 01480 472545;
Squires Kitchen, Squires House, 3 Waverley Lane, Farnham, Surrey, GU9 8BB, Tel: 01252 711749.
Hannah's Chocolate and Sugarcraft Shop, 10 Barrow Rd, Quorn, Leicestershire, LE12 8DL, Tel: 01509 416638

NOTES ON USING THE RECIPES
For all recipes, quantities are given in metric, Imperial and cup measurements. Follow one set of measures only as they are not interchangeable. Standard 5ml teaspoons (tsp) and 15ml tablespoons (tbsp) are used. Australian readers, whose tablespoons measure 20ml, should adjust quantities accordingly. All spoon measures are assumed to be level unless otherwise stated.
Eggs are a standard size 3 (medium) unless otherwise stated.

CONTENTS

INTRODUCTION

Although I work in all areas of sugarcraft, chocolate is my favourite. With chocolate, an array of wonderful creations can be made in a short time using basic equipment. These creations make ideal gifts for a variety of occasions, although if you are a chocoholic like me, you will enjoy eating them any day of the week!

I have been working with chocolate for around ten years, demonstrating and teaching around the country. During this time I have met many people who are fascinated by chocolate but have been put off working with it either because they have dabbled unsuccessfully or they are frightened by the processes of tempering and the various temperatures involved. I decided that a book was needed to teach a basic understanding of working with chocolate, with easy to follow step-by-step explanations of the tempering process and the techniques used by the chocolatier to create pieces ranging from a simple chocolate animal to exquisite centrepieces.

So here it is – now there is no excuse. Read on, buy some chocolate, lock yourself in the kitchen, let your imagination run riot and enjoy yourself!

THE STORY OF CHOCOLATE

Archaeologists believe that the cocoa tree may be over four thousand years old, and came from the Orinoco and Amazon regions of South Amazon. Our first knowledge of the tree comes from the Aztecs, who in their migrations through the subcontinent probably brought the tree to Yucatan at around 600 A.D. Here the Mayas established the earliest known plantation for growing cocoa.

The cocoa tree produces large oval yellow pods, each containing around 30 cocoa beans. These beans played an important role in the lives of the early Central and South American peoples. The Aztecs, Mayas and the Incas all attributed magical powers to the cocoa bean and it was also used as currency. Its most important function however, was culinary. The beans were roasted, ground, and combined with liquid to make a drink called *xocotlatl*.

It was Christopher Columbus who in 1502 had the distinction of being the first European to discover cocoa beans, followed by Spanish conquistadors Cortez and Pizarro, who established plantations and sent the crop to their native Spain. The chocolate drink became popular with the Spanish aristocracy who mixed it with vanilla and cinnamon. It was kept a secret for nearly a century before it found its way to France where it soon became fashionable. It then spread to the rest of Europe and by the 18th century it was served in coffee houses throughout England.

The first chocolates were made in Germany in 1663, when the cook of a wealthy Augsburg trader designed a special delicacy made from almonds, dates and marzipan, covered in chocolate. He called it 'Praline'.

Chocolate was attributed with healing properties and sold by chemists to cure consumptives and gastric patients. It was also said to have aphrodisiac powers which were touted by Madame du Barry, who fed it to her boyfriends. Casanova seduced countless women with its help.

At this time chocolate was still prepared by hand, but in 1795 Dr Joseph Fry started chocolate manufacture on a large scale, using a steam engine to grind the beans. In 1928 a Dutch chocolate maker invented the cocoa press which squeezed the cocoa butter from the beans, making a smoother and more appetizing drink. Drinking chocolate was beginning to develop a refined taste similar to today's drink.

The two most important developments in chocolate, however, took place in Switzerland. In 1875, after years of experimentation, Daniel Peter succeeded in adding condensed milk to chocolate to produce a solid milk chocolate for eating. In 1879 Rodolphe Lindt invented 'conching' – a new method of refining to produce a much smoother chocolate which could be poured into moulds, paving the way for making chocolates as we know them today.

FROM COCOA TREE TO CHOCOLATE FACTORY

One of the reasons that chocolate is such a precious commodity is that the cocoa tree is extremely sensitive. It thrives only in a tropical climate with intense heat and moisture. Therefore, its cultivation is limited to areas near the equator – Central and northern South America, central and west Africa and parts of South East Asia.

Due to their delicate nature, cocoa trees start their life indoors before transplanting to

6

plantations protected from direct sunlight by larger trees such as banana and coconut. In their second year blossoms appear not on the branches but on the trunk. By their third and fourth years they are bearing ripe fruit in the form of pods, which are picked by using large knives tied to poles to reach the high pods. The pods are split and the beans removed. The beans are beige in colour but take on a purplish hue when exposed to the air.

The beans are then heaped together and covered with leaves and fermented for up to nine days to remove any bitterness. During this process, bacteria ferments sugar in the pulp which causes heat, killing germinating capabilities and unleashing enzymes that develop flavour. At the end of this process the beans have at last turned brown. They are now treated to a week of sunbathing to dry them out, after which they turn a deeper brown and develop a richer fragrance. They are then packed in sacks ready for transportation to the next stage – the chocolate factory.

THE CHOCOLATE FACTORY

After cleaning and sorting, the beans are roasted similarly to coffee beans, when they become even darker in colour and take on their evocative 'chocolate' aroma. After cooling, the hard shells are removed in a crushing machine, leaving the cocoa meat or 'nibs'.

These nibs are ground to a fine paste in rollers which generate intense heat, melting the cocoa butter and creating a thick liquid known as 'chocolate liquor'. Here, some of the liquor is put through a hydraulic press to extract the cocoa butter. The remaining cakes are crushed and sieved to produce cocoa powder. When

Easter eggs are a popular novelty, see page 38.

sugar is added it becomes the basis for hot chocolate: the modern version of *xocotlatl*.

The rest of the liquor goes to make the chocolate we eat: cocoa butter and sugar are mixed in to form a doughy, gritty substance which tastes good but is not smooth. Milk chocolate has milk solids added at the mixing stage. White chocolate consists of cocoa butter, sugar and milk solids. It contains no cocoa liquor so is not true chocolate but it behaves like chocolate due to the cocoa butter. The mixture is ground further by heavy rollers and then refined by the 'conching' process. This involves placing the chocolate into large troughs where it is heated and passed through rollers continually for two or more days. At last! The chocolate has that smooth, melt-on-your tongue quality. It is then tempered and moulded into blocks, drops or bars and wrapped and packaged.

TYPES OF CHOCOLATE

A huge variety of chocolate bars with household names such as Cadburys and Rowntrees grace the shelves in nearly every store. Although they taste very good, they are not suitable for melting and using for chocolate work as they are often mixtures of different fats and will not set properly.

COUVERTURE is the correct chocolate for use by the chocolatier.

It contains a high percentage of cocoa butter and is designed for moulding and chocolate making. It has a good gloss and sets hard (referred to as 'snap'). There is a comprehensive range of couvertures available for use by the professional, depending on the equipment used and the job in hand. Thicker couvertures are for hand dipping whilst thinner types are available for use with machinery.

DARK COUVERTURE comes in varying degrees of bitterness – from sweet through to extra bitter depending on the amounts of cocoa solids and sugar added.

MILK COUVERTURE can be bought in various shades – from very creamy and pale to almost dark.

WHITE COUVERTURE also comes in various types including different colours.

Because of the cocoa butter content, couverture requires tempering before use (see page 12). This is a process that allows the chocolate to set in the desired crystalline form. Couverture can be purchased from specialist suppliers and chocolatiers, in blocks or drops. Look for the best-quality when buying, such as Callebaut from Belgium or Cocoa Barry from France. Make sure it has been stored correctly and not left open to the atmosphere to absorb moisture and odours.

BAKER'S CHOCOLATE was designed as a soft cutting chocolate for use by bakers to coat cakes that could be cut without splintering. It is produced by removing the hard cocoa butter and replacing it with a softer vegetable fat. Because it contains no cocoa butter it does not require tempering before use – just melt and use. It is not used by the chocolatier as it lacks flavour, gloss and snap.

COOKING CHOCOLATE is a cheaper alternative to couverture for general use as a flavouring. Again, not used by the chocolatier.

THERMOMETERS Because of the need to measure temperatures accurately, a good thermometer is essential. Several types are available. A basic thermometer is the small pocket type, reading up to 60°C (140°F). Although they can be a degree or two out, they are inexpensive and as long as you allow for inaccuracy, are usually ample for the amateur.

● For the professional, the digital type with probe is essential. Precise temperatures can be measured and are easily read on the display.

MICROWAVE OVEN OR DOUBLE BOILING PAN A microwave oven is a handy piece of equipment for melting and warming chocolate quickly and cleanly. If you do not have one a good double boiling pan will do the same job.

MOULDS Although many chocolate items can be made without the use of moulds, they are used for a great deal of pieces.

● Moulds come in many shapes and sizes; they also vary in quality.

● There is a vast selection of inexpensive, thin plastic moulds available from sugarcraft shops which can give good results if looked after (they are easily broken or warped if washed in water that is too hot).

● For the professional who needs to use equipment over and over again, thick plastic moulds can be ordered from specialist suppliers. They are expensive but are very strong and will last many years if looked after. Don't go for cheap versions of these professional moulds made from thinner plastics as they warp easily and do not give a neat finish. Also look out for neat, sharp definition in the mould as this will be transferred to the chocolate being moulded.

Types of moulds are described in more detail on page 18.

BAIN MARIES AND TEMPERING MACHINES A piece of equipment that will keep the chocolate at the correct working temperature is very useful as it gives you a much longer time with which to work with the chocolate.

● Special equipment can be bought which utilizes either water or air that is thermostatically controlled to keep the chocolate at the correct temperature. This equipment is very expensive. A good substitute can be made from a bain marie and a tropical fish tank thermometer.

OTHER EQUIPMENT If you are a sugarcrafter, you will probably already own most of the necessary small equipment. If not, your local sugarcraft shop will be only too pleased to help you. The following equipment is used in this book:

● A good metal side scraper and palette knife
● Thick plastic scrapers – straight and comb styles
● Plastic chopping board and small rolling pin
● A selection of flower and leaf cutters
● Acetate sheets
● Pastry brushes and small paintbrushes
● Scissors and knives
● Greaseproof paper (parchment)

Most of the other equipment consists of bits of plastic, bubblewrap, buckets, tubs, bowls and anything lying around the kitchen which looks the right size or shape for moulding. I have even been known to dismantle light fittings in order to use the patterns on chocolate bases!

The word 'tempering' is used in many industries. It means heat processing a material – such as steel – to bring it to a desired crystalline state. This definition also applies to chocolate couverture. It is tempered so that the final solid product will have a particular crystalline form – that is, a good gloss, and a hard structure with a good snap when broken.

● To work with couverture, an understanding of the basic theory of the tempering process is important. When a liquid is cooled, it remains a liquid until it reaches its solidification point. Then it begins to crystallize until the whole has become solid. In chocolate, cocoa and sugar solids are suspended in cocoa butter. When cocoa butter cools it can crystallize in several solid forms. The main two forms we will call Fat A and Fat B.

● Fat A is a soft greasy fat and has a low melting point.

● Fat B is a more stable fat and has a higher melting point which gives the chocolate its glossy finish and brittle snap.

● To temper we have to eliminate the A crystals and leave behind the B crystals. When the chocolate solidifies it will then follow the pattern of B crystals because they are the only type present.

● To do this we make use of the difference in melting point between the two types of fat crystals, see chart on page 13.

● The couverture is now tempered once the soft A type crystals have been eliminated.

● If the chocolate crystallizes incorrectly in the A type crystals, then it will slowly transform into the B state, but in doing so will show the characteristics of untempered chocolate – streakiness, blotchiness and a general bad finish.

● The next problem now arises – the tempered couverture must be kept at the working temperature of 32°C (89°F) and used as soon as possible. It must not be allowed to exceed 34°C (93°F) as the B type crystals will melt, and cause it to be untempered. On the other hand if it cools too much, it will be difficult to work with. Because 32°C (89°F) is below the solidification point of B crystals, they will gradually keep forming, making the couverture become thicker and thicker. One of the terms for this is 'going puddingy'.

MILK COUVERTURE

Milk couverture contains a proportion of dairy fat which has a lower melting point and is softer than cocoa butter and results in the softening of the cocoa butter. This means that milk couverture must be used at a slightly lower temperature than plain, around 30–31°C (85–87°F).

WHITE COUVERTURE

White couverture is made from cocoa fat, sugar and milk solids. As it contains no cocoa solids it can be said that it is not true chocolate. However, as it contains cocoa butter it behaves like chocolate, and as it contains a high percentage of milk solids, the working temperature for white chocolate must be lower; around 28–29°C (83–85°F).

The shine and gloss on this snowman are achieved by correct tempering.

TEMPERING PLAIN COUVERTURE

❖

Temperature	**Fat A** soft/greasy low melting point about 28°C (83°F)	**Fat B** hard/brittle high melting point about 34°C (93°F)
Melt to 45°C (113°F)	All liquid	All liquid
Cool to 26°C (79°F)	Crystals form	Crystals form
Warm to 32°C (89°F)	Crystals melt	Crystals still present

DIFFERENT METHODS OF MELTING

❖

If using block couverture, melting will be quicker if it is first chopped into small pieces. Use only clean, dry, and odour-free tools and boards. It is easier to use couverture in chip or drop form as it is difficult to chop up.

The first stage of the tempering process is to melt the chocolate. The melting process can be done in any of the following ways:

IN A BAIN MARIE OR DOUBLE BOILER Heat the water. Do not boil to avoid steam – 60°C (140°F) is ideal. Place the bowl of couverture in the bain marie. The bowl should fit the bain marie perfectly to avoid water getting into the chocolate.

IN A MICROWAVE Set the microwave on a low setting and switch on for a minute at a time, stirring in between, until fully melted. Do not leave the spoon in the bowl during the melting process as it may cause the chocolate to burn.

IN A TEMPERING MACHINE Couverture can be melted in a tempering machine or overnight in a warming cupboard. Make sure the warming cupboard is dry and without ventilation or crusting will occur.

Before attempting to chop block chocolate, leave it in a warm place for a while. Use a large knife and slice off shavings from the edge.

When melting chocolate in a bain marie, keep the water below boiling point to avoid steam. Stir the chocolate gently with a metal spoon.

THE MARBLING METHOD OF TEMPERING PLAIN COUVERTURE USING DROPS OR BLOCK

❖

For milk couverture, melt to 43°C (113°F) and cool to 30–31°C (86–87°F)

For white couverture, melt to 43°C (109°F) and cool to 28–29°C (83–85°F)

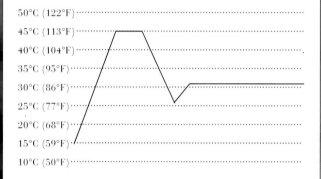

```
50°C (122°F) ·········································
45°C (113°F) ·········································
40°C (104°F) ·········································
35°C (95°F)  ·········································
30°C (86°F)  ·········································
25°C (77°F)  ·········································
20°C (68°F)  ·········································
15°C (59°F)  ·········································
10°C (50°F)  ·········································
```

NOTE If the couverture is allowed to cool too much it cannot be brought back to the correct temperature by simply warming up. The couverture is too thick and can only be corrected by melting and tempering again.

~ 1 ~

Melt the couverture in a bowl until it is at a temperature of 45°C (113°F) and completely melted. Stir well. Pour two thirds of the couverture onto a marble slab to cool. Spread out and collect to the centre with a palette knife. Continue until it begins to thicken.

~ 2 ~

Scrape up the mixture and return to the bowl with the remaining warm couverture and stir well (do not beat). Measure the temperature. It should be 32°C (89°F). If necessary, adjust the temperature of the couverture by cooling or warming slightly.

THE VACCINATION METHOD OF TEMPERING PLAIN COUVERTURE USING DROPS

❖

For milk couverture, melt to 43°C (113°F) and cool to 30–31°C (86–87°F)

For white couverture, melt to 43°C (109°F) and cool to 28–29°C (83–85°F)

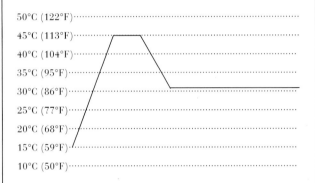

50°C (122°F)
45°C (113°F)
40°C (104°F)
35°C (95°F)
30°C (86°F)
25°C (77°F)
20°C (68°F)
15°C (59°F)
10°C (50°F)

NOTE If the couverture is allowed to cool too much it cannot be brought back to the correct temperature by simply warming up. The couverture is too thick and can only be corrected by melting and tempering again.

~ 1 ~

Melt the couverture in a bowl until it is at a temperature of 45°C (113°F) and completely melted. Stir well. Sprinkle in some drops and stir until melted. Do not add too many at once as the temperature will drop too fast, they will not melt and the mixture will be lumpy.

~ 2 ~

Measure the temperature. Add some more drops, stir and measure temperature. Continue until the temperature is lowered to 32°C (89°F) and the mixture is smooth. If the temperature drops below 32°C (89°F) it can be warmed up slightly.

IMPORTANT TIPS AND ADVICE FOR SUCCESS

● Store chocolate at around 18°C (65°F).

● As chocolate easily absorbs moisture, keep in a dry place in an airtight container. Reseal packets after use.

● Chocolate is sensitive to foreign odours so keep away from strong-smelling foods and substances.

● White chocolate is light-sensitive so store in the dark as it will fade if exposed to light.

● Do not let water or steam come into contact with the chocolate. It will cause it to thicken, rendering it useless for working. Chocolate in this state can, however, be used for cooking and fillings.

● If couverture is kept liquid for a several days, the cocoa butter and the solids will separate. Stir the couverture two or three times a day or let it set after use.

● Use only the best couverture for chocolate work. Never mix other chocolates with couverture as vegetable fats have a negative influence on the shine.

● Do not let the couverture heat above 50°C (122°F) at any time.

If the weather is very damp or humid do not attempt to work with chocolate. Wait until it dries out and the humidity is lower.

● For perfect results, keep to the correct temperatures whilst tempering and working. Your working room should be an average room temperature. A cooler room should be available for setting items.

● Take care to prepare moulds and acetates correctly. (See page 18.)

● Do not rush. Be patient, especially when waiting for chocolate to release itself from moulds. If you try and help it along you will leave marks and dull patches on the surface of the chocolate.

● Make sure your hands, moulds and equipment are totally clean and dry before starting work. Any grease will mark the shiny surface and look unsightly.

● Chocolate can be thickened by the addition of glycerine or water. Add a drop at a time until the correct consistency is achieved. Use immediately - do not return any leftover to the ordinary melted chocolate. Thickened chocolate can be used for piping (see page 55) or as a filling etc.

USING MOULDS FOR CHOCOLATE

$\mathcal{B}$efore starting, it is very important to prepare the moulds properly. Begin by washing in warm soapy water and rinsing. Dry thoroughly and polish with a soft dry cloth or cotton wool pads.

NOTE Any grease or dirt in the mould will cause marks and dull patches, and make the chocolate difficult to demould.

● Any traces of water in the mould will cause severe white marks on the chocolate, so ensure that the moulds are completely dry.

● Moulds should be at room temperature before filling with chocolate. If they are too cold, it will cause the chocolate to go dull.

● Have a cool room available for filled moulds to enable them to set quickly. Good air circulation is important to remove heat rapidly.

● Do not put the filled moulds in a refrigerator for too long. They can cool too quickly, causing the shapes to crack. Also, if they become too cold they will develop condensation when removed from the cold into the warm. This will cause dullness due to sugar bloom (see Faults and Corrections, pages 66–67).

TYPES OF MOULD USED IN THIS BOOK

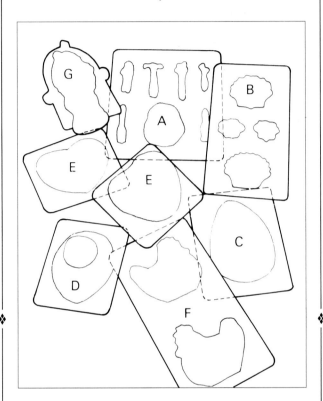

A thin plastic moulds
B sea shell moulds
C egg mould
D basket mould
E heart box mould
F chicken mould
G clip-together plastic mould

EXPERT ADVICE
≈

Always buy the best quality moulds you can afford. The finished item is only as good as the mould it came out of.

MOULDING SIMPLE SOLID SHAPES

*S*olid shapes are the easiest chocolate pieces to produce, so they make a good starting point for the beginner. There are hundreds of moulds on the market which produce an array of novelty figures for Easter, Christmas, Valentine's Day, Mother's Day and so on. Some moulds may make more than one piece but the method is the same. They could be gift wrapped, see page 68, or used as an edible decoration on a cake.

FILLING A LARGE ONE-PIECE MOULD

❖

In the example top right, I have made a golf bag which would make an ideal Father's Day or Easter gift for a golfing fanatic.

FILLING A MOULD FULL OF SMALL SHAPES

❖

Children love small chocolate novelties. Some moulds are very versatile as they provide a number of different shapes in one go. These can be gift wrapped and used as stocking fillers at Christmas time or as Easter gifts.

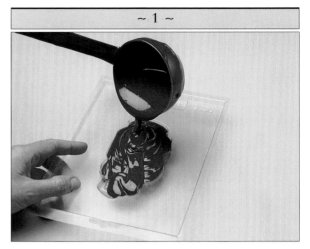

~ 1 ~

FILLING A LARGE ONE-PIECE MOULD Temper the chocolate and prepare the mould. Carefully pour the chocolate into the mould until it reaches the top. Try not to let it overflow. Tap the mould gently on the table to remove any air bubbles. Leave to set in a cool room.

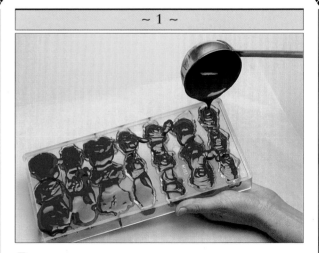

~ 1 ~

FILLING A MOULD FULL OF SMALL SHAPES With a ladle, pour chocolate into the centre of the mould and trickle it over all the shapes to be filled.

~ 2 ~

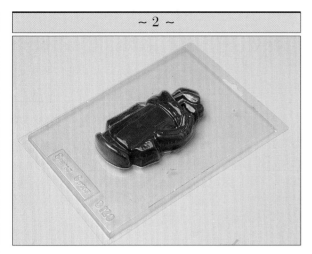

As the chocolate cools and sets it contracts. It will therefore come away from the mould on its own. You can see this happen; the shiny parts have come away, the darker areas have not.

~ 3 ~

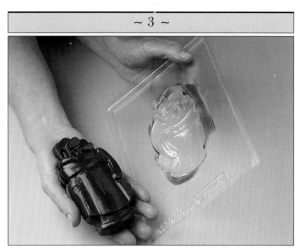

When it has completely come away from the mould, tip it upside-down and the shape should fall out. Sometimes a gentle tap is needed. Do not try to force the chocolate from the mould as it will leave marks on the surface.

~ 2 ~

Using a plastic scraper, push the chocolate into all the indentations. Scrape off the excess chocolate from the top and sides of the mould.

~ 3 ~

Tap the mould on the table to remove air bubbles from the chocolate and leave to set. Remove from the mould in the same way as for the one-piece mould.

~ ❖ ~

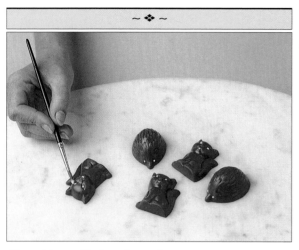

To add small details such as eyes, use a small paintbrush and dab a dot of chocolate in place. Leave to dry thoroughly before gift wrapping.

~ ❖ ~

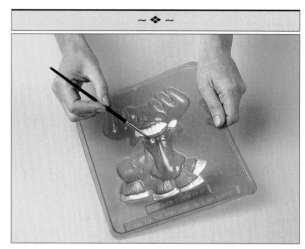

Use a larger brush or piping bag to fill larger areas of a mould such as this moose. Leave each colour to set before filling as usual.

ADDING HIGHLIGHTS

Different-coloured chocolate can be used to highlight certain parts of a novelty piece which otherwise would be difficult to see, such as Rudolph's eyes and hat, Santa's beard, bunny's tail and teeth (see page 27).

ADDING EMPHASIS

Colour can also be added to make a piece more appealing, such as turning a plain dog into a spotty dog. Dark chocolate can be painted onto milk or white chocolate, and vice versa, to emphasize certain areas.

MAKING A HOLLOW SHAPE

*T*here are two ways of making hollow shapes. Method 1 uses commercial moulds consisting of two halves which clip together producing a one-piece hollow figure. Method 2 uses moulds in two separate halves. The chocolate pieces are joined together when set. (See key on page 18.)

~ 1 ~

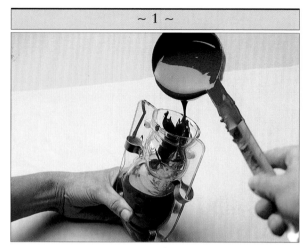

METHOD 1 Polish and clip the moulds together. Fill the mould to the top with chocolate. Be careful not to get chocolate on the outside of the mould as it is wasteful and hinders removal of the mould later. Tap the mould on the table to remove air bubbles.

~ 1 ~

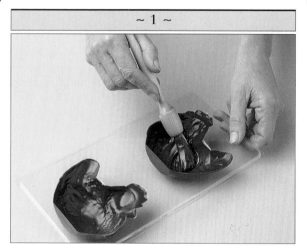

METHOD 2 Pour some chocolate into the two halves of the mould and, using a pastry brush, spread it into all the nooks and crannies. Make sure there is plenty of chocolate around the inside of the lip to form a thicker edge (they will join together more neatly).

~ 2 ~

Place the mould upside-down on a flat surface. Leave to set. Repeat the procedure to give another coat. Hold the mould up to the light. If any light can be seen through the chocolate it is too thin. Brush some more chocolate on these areas.

~ 2 ~

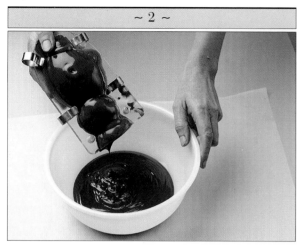

Tip the mould upside-down and pour out the chocolate until it stops. Wipe the base and place on greaseproof paper. Leave in a cool place. When set, repeat the procedure. If necessary, cut away some of the chocolate in the base before pouring in the second coat.

~ 3 ~

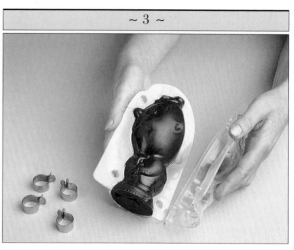

Leave to set until it comes away from mould. Remove the clips, prise the two halves of the mould apart and lift out the chocolate figure. If one half is reluctant to come out, tip upside-down and flex the mould.

~ 3 ~

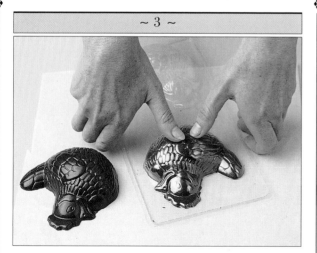

When set and the chocolate has come away from the mould, tap or flex the mould to remove the two halves.

~ 4 ~

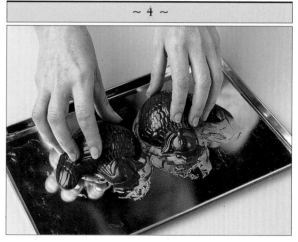

To join the halves together, warm a metal tray and place them on for a few seconds until the edges soften and start to melt. Remove quickly and stick together. Leave to set.

VARIATIONS

When you have mastered the use of these moulds, you may like to try some variations by using chocolate in more than one colour. The process is similar to using solid-piece moulds, except that the detail is painted on before the moulds are clipped together.

Using a paintbrush, paint in details in dark chocolate and leave to set. Clip the moulds together then fill with white chocolate as usual.

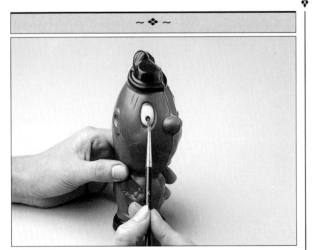

Here is an example of using all three shades of chocolate. Small details such as eyes and buttons can be painted on afterwards.

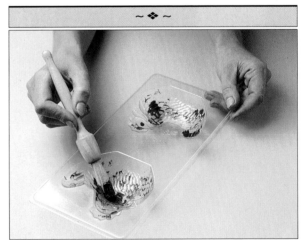

Another effect is to use a large brush to add texture to moulds. Dip the brush in dark chocolate and brush lightly over the chicken's feathers to highlight them. Leave to set, then fill the mould with white chocolate, as usual.

CHICKEN IN A BASKET

*T*his is a delightful gift for a child at Easter and is made using basic techniques and inexpensive moulds. The basket can be filled with mini-eggs, chocolate novelties or sweets. The hollow chicken is made from white chocolate, see page 25, but the mould is textured in dark chocolate first, see page 26, to highlight the feathers. Fill the basket with chocolate shavings, see page 58, and place mini-eggs around the edge. Finally, position the chicken on top of the eggs and gift wrap if wished, see page 68.

~ 1 ~

TO MAKE THE BASKET *Polish the basket mould and temper the chocolate. Spoon some chocolate into the mould and, using a pastry brush, spread it evenly around the mould.*

~ 2 ~

Run your thumb around the rim of the mould to make a neat edge. Leave to set. When set, brush another coat of chocolate into the mould and leave in a cool room until it releases itself from the mould. To free the basket, slight pressure might be needed on the base of the mould.

EXPERT ADVICE

≈

If wished, the chicken itself could also be filled with small eggs and chocolate novelties, see page 39, step 6.

CHOCOLATE LEAVES

*T*he most effective way to make chocolate leaves is to use real leaves as a mould. Look for thick leaves with a smooth back and a good vein. If the underside is furry, the chocolate will not peel off when set. Make sure that the leaves are not poisonous or dirty. Always wash them well and dry thoroughly, then gently polish with a cotton wool pad.

Get into the habit of keeping an eye open for interesting-looking leaves whenever you are out walking – they are extremely useful for chocolate work!

~ 1 ~

Brush a thin coat of chocolate onto the underside of the leaves. Leave to set hard.

~ 2 ~

Peel the leaf very carefully off the chocolate (do not attempt to peel the chocolate off the leaf) and store for later use. The leaves can be re-polished and used again.

EXPERT ADVICE

≈

The finished leaves are extremely thin and delicate. Keep them in a cool place to ensure they do not melt or break.

MODELLING CHOCOLATE

Also known as plastic or leather chocolate due to its appearance, modelling chocolate is made by blending couverture with glucose syrup. Various shades can be created by using white, milk and dark chocolate. White modelling chocolate can also be dyed in primary colours by using strong paste colours. It can be made in advance, wrapped and stored in an airtight container or frozen until required. The recipe below can be used to model flowers, animals and so on, in the same way as marzipan (almond paste).

MODELLING CHOCOLATE

500g (1 lb) couverture
250g (8 oz) glucose syrup

Melt the couverture in a double boiler or microwave to approximately to 32°C (89°F). Warm the glucose syrup to approximately the same temperature. Mix the two together and stir. The mixture will start to curdle.

Take a handful at a time and squeeze over a clean bowl. The cocoa butter will separate and drip out.

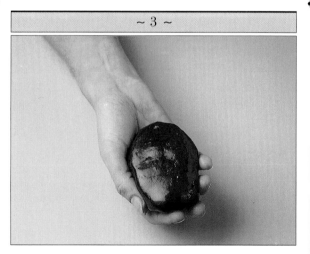

Keep squeezing until the paste is smooth. Wrap it in a plastic bag and leave to cool and firm up. It is then ready to use. If the paste becomes too cold it will set harder and be difficult to work with. Warm it in the microwave or hot plate and knead until soft again.

CHOCOLATE ROSES

*M*odelling chocolate is a wonderful medium to work with. Beautiful flowers can be created without tools or cutters. The rose is a good flower to start with as it can be used to decorate so many chocolate cakes and centrepieces. To prepare the paste, simply warm it gently and knead until a consistency similar to plasticine is achieved. The warmer it is, the softer it will be. The consistency can also be varied by altering the recipe slightly. Add more glucose to produce a softer setting paste and more chocolate to produce a harder paste.

A calyx may be added to the rose if wished. Roll out some paste and cut out with a rose calyx cutter. Stick to the base of the rose with a little chocolate. Try using paste colours to colour the white modelling chocolate. Yellows, pinks and greens can add a new dimension to a chocolate piece.

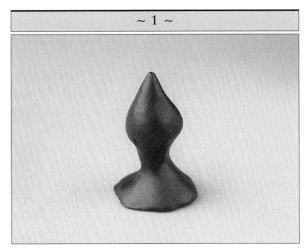

~ 1 ~

Take a ball of modelling chocolate and fashion it into a shape resembling a rosebud on a stem. Leave sufficient paste attached to form a base.

~ 4 ~

Wrap a petal around the bud, leaving one side curled back. Tuck another petal into the gap and wrap around to join on other side. Remould the base of the bud and pull down the edges of the petals to form an unfurling rosebud.

EXPERT ADVICE

≈

If you have naturally hot hands this may cause difficulties. Try making all the petals first and laying them on a cold surface before making up the rose.

~ 2 ~

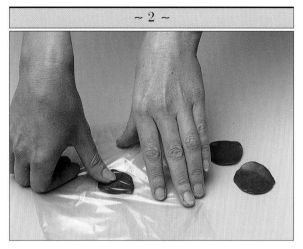

To make the petals, mould smooth balls of paste about the size of a hazelnut. Place between two sheets of polythene and, using your thumb, press gently, working from the centre out, to form a petal shape which is very thin on the edge and thicker in the middle.

~ 3 ~

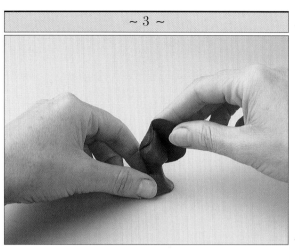

Wrap the first petal around the bud so it completely covers the tip. At each stage, re-mould the base of the bud to keep the original shape.

~ 5 ~

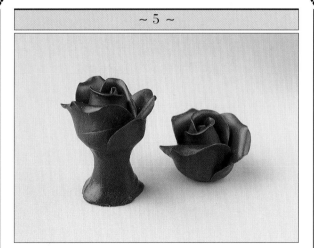

The next stage uses three petals. One by one, attach them to the side of the bud and wrap around, leaving one edge curled back. Reform the base of the rose and pull down the edges of the petals to form a rose shape. The rose can now be severed just below the base.

~ 6 ~

To make a full rose, add another four petals in the same way. Normally one full rose is used as the centre of a display, surrounded by smaller roses and buds.

RIBBONS AND BOWS

Chocolate rosettes, ribbons and bows look breathtaking when used to decorate a gâteau, Easter egg or plaque. It may take a while to perfect the technique shown right, but the effort is worthwhile. The plain acetate pieces can be washed, polished and re-used. When you have mastered the technique, try experimenting with different colours and textures (see below).

~ 1 ~

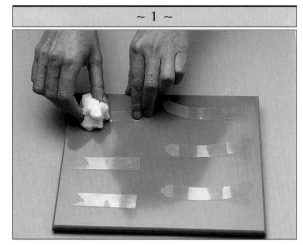

Using the templates on page 36, cut the acetate into the required shapes. Lay on a marble slab or flat surface and polish clean. Temper the chocolate and, using a palette knife, spread a thin even coat over the acetate. Make sure there are no very thin areas.

Various patterned acetates can be purchased which transfer their patterns onto the chocolate when peeled off, as with the gold flecks shown here. Apply the same method as described above. Spread the chocolate on the printed side. Note – these acetates can only be used once.

This pattern is achieved by spinning white chocolate backwards and forwards over the acetate and waiting until it is just setting. Spread on dark chocolate and continue as described above. The colours can be reversed – spin dark chocolate and spread on white.

~ 2 ~

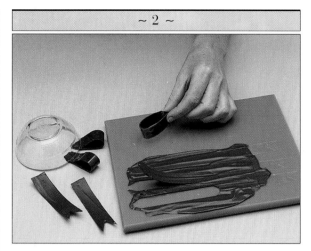

Lift the edges of the acetate with a blade and leave to set on greaseproof paper (parchment). To make the loops, press the ends together before the chocolate sets. If they spring back open, place on a small weight to hold them together.

~ 3 ~

When set, peel away the acetate. Trim the ends, dip into melted chocolate and arrange to form gift bows.

A marbled effect is created by using two shades of chocolate. Brush dark chocolate onto the acetate and immediately pour on some white. Using a pastry brush, swirl the chocolate round in random circular movements, pressing firmly. Use a palette knife to spread it evenly.

To create a striped ribbon, spread dark chocolate over the acetate strips and pull a comb scraper through to form small grooves. When just setting, pour on a little white chocolate and level with a palette knife. Continue as described above.

VALENTINE'S DAY HEART-SHAPED BOX

*W*hat better way to say 'I love you' than to present somebody special with this beautiful box, filled with their favourite chocolates?

heart-shaped box mould and lid
about 250g (8 oz) dark couverture
60g (2 oz) dark modelling chocolate
125g (4 oz) white modelling chocolate
125g (4 oz) chocolates to fill the box
4 ribbon loops and two tails cut from acetate
(see templates, right)

⬤ Temper some dark chocolate and polish the moulds.

⬤ To make the heart-shaped box, follow the instructions for the basket on page 28. The lid is a thin solid shape so just pour a little chocolate into the mould, tap it on the table to remove air bubbles and leave to set.

⬤ While the box is setting, make the bow loops and tails from white chocolate marbled with dark. See instructions on page 34.

⬤ Make a large chocolate rose from the dark modelling chocolate, see page 32.

⬤ Carefully remove the box and lid from the moulds.

⬤ Arrange the bow on top of the lid and stick down with a little chocolate. Stick the rose in the centre.

⬤ Fill the box with about 125g (4 oz) best quality chocolates.

⬤ Gift wrap if required, see page 68, and present to your loved one.

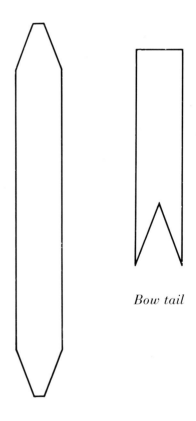

Bow tail

Bow loop

EXPERT ADVICE
≈

The dark chocolate could be substituted with milk or white chocolate to make contrasting roses and bows.

CHOCOLATE EGGS

*E*aster eggs are the most popular chocolate novelty today, but the shop-bought variety can be prohibitively expensive. It's rewarding and much more fun to produce your own beautiful creations using the simplest of moulds and a little imagination. The eggs can be filled with chocolate novelties or left hollow.

~ 1 ~

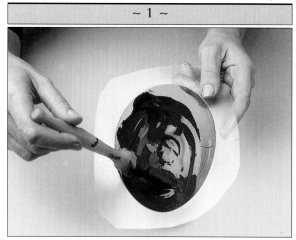

Pour chocolate into the egg mould and, using a brush, spread it evenly around the mould, pushing extra chocolate around the edge to form a lip.

~ 4 ~

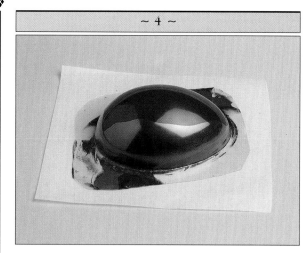

Leave to set in a cool area until the chocolate has released itself from the mould. When it is ready it will appear shiny.

EXPERT ADVICE

≈

When choosing an egg mould, pick one with a neat edge, which is not curved. You will get a much neater join. Crackled pattern moulds look lovely in one colour but plain shells look better if you wish to create your own patterns.

~ 2 ~

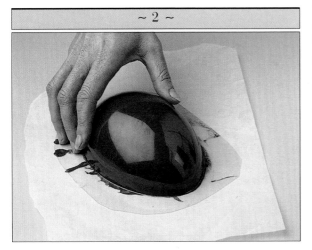

Quickly tip the mould upside-down onto greaseproof paper (parchment) on a flat tray. Run your thumb around the mould to press it down hard onto the paper and leave to set.

~ 3 ~

Brush in another coat of chocolate. Hold the mould up to bright light. If you can see light through, brush in more chocolate until no light shows.

~ 5 ~

Gently remove the egg from the mould. Sometimes gentle pressure is needed to remove the egg as static electricity can hold it in.

~ 6 ~

To join the two halves together, warm a metal tray and place the egg halves on for a few seconds until they start to soften and melt around the edge. Remove and join together. Leave to set. Fillings such as chocolates or a small toy can be placed inside prior to joining.

THE MARBLED EGG Brush in a small amount of dark or milk chocolate and, while still wet, pour in white chocolate. With a brush, swirl it round, pushing firmly until the whole mould is covered. Leave to set. For the second coat, brush in any colour.

THE STIPPLED EGG Dip a piece of stippling sponge in dark or milk chocolate and gently dab on greaseproof paper (parchment) to remove excess. Gently dab on the mould until covered all over. Leave to set. Fill with white chocolate as usual.

THE SPECKLED EGG *Dip a stencil brush into dark chocolate and flick the end to create small speckles in the mould. Leave to set. Fill with white chocolate as usual.*

THE FEATHERED EGG *Fill a small greaseproof paper (parchment) piping bag with dark chocolate and cut a small hole in the tip. Pipe a criss-cross pattern on the inside of the mould and leave to set. Continue filling with white or milk chocolate as usual.*

BASES AND BACKGROUNDS

For a centrepiece or display a base is needed on which the figures or eggs can be arranged. Backgrounds can also be added to make the figure stand out.

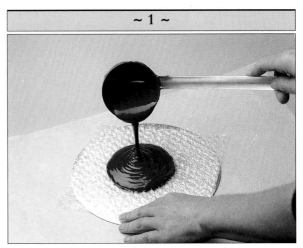

BASES *The simplest way to make a base is to pour chocolate onto patterned plastic (clean dry bubblewrap or the patterned perspex used in light diffusers is ideal).*

If a more precise base shape is needed, cut the shape out of a large sheet of chocolate. Gently push a warm cutter through the chocolate and wipe off the melted excess. Do not push too hard or the chocolate will crack.

~ 2 ~

Spread the chocolate with a palette knife to the desired shape between 3-6mm (⅛–¼ in) thick and then tap on the table to remove air bubbles. Leave to set in a cool room.

~ 3 ~

When set hard, turn upside-down and peel off the bubblewrap. Hold the base firmly to prevent it snapping. Bases set on a sheet of perspex are removed by flexing the perspex down away from the base.

~ ❖ ~

To obtain squares and rectangles, cut gently with a hot knife. Again, wipe off any melted chocolate as it will bloom when it sets.

EXPERT ADVICE
≈

As moulded pieces are smooth, they will stand out better if the base and backgrounds are textured or in a contrasting colour. Keep an eye open for unusual patterned plastic such as bubblewraps and packing cases.

~ 1 ~

BACKGROUNDS *To make a curved background, spread chocolate over an acetate sheet to the desired shape using a palette knife.*

~ 2 ~

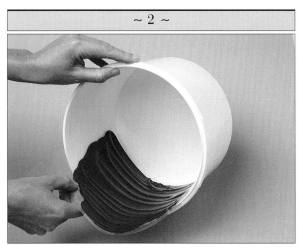

Place the sheet inside a tub or large tube to obtain the curved shape. Leave to set slowly (if it cools too fast it will curl up or even crack).

~ 3 ~

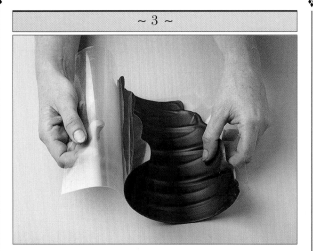

When set hard, gently peel off the acetate sheet. Handle with care as the chocolate is thin and very delicate.

~ 4 ~

Dip the background in chocolate and glue to the base. If the base is not straight, gently melt on a warm tray until it is level.

When you have mastered the basic technique, experiment with different textures and colours.

On the right, different-coloured chocolates are brushed on quickly in succession to give a colourful effect. The acetate is then taped to the outside of the tub so the pattern is on the shiny inside of the curve.

On the left, a see-through effect is created. Fill a piping bag with chocolate and cut the end with scissors equal to a no. 2 piping tube (tip). Start piping circles on the acetate continuously until the whole shape is covered in overlapping circles. Lay in the tub and leave to set.

EASTER EGG CENTREPIECE

*T*his exquisite centrepiece uses all the various techniques used in chocolate work and would make a truly stunning centrepiece for an Easter table. Surrounded by a dark chocolate rope, the softly marbled egg is seen against a delicate piped background which contrasts superbly with the solidity of the dark chocolate base and white ribbons and bows. Dark chocolate roses complete the effect. Add a few of your own ideas to make a truly impressive gift.

1 base made from dark couverture, either cutout or random shape, see page 42
1 curved background made from dark couverture, see page 44
2 Easter egg shells, 1 plain and 1 patterned, see page 38
1 large rose, 2 smaller roses and 2 rosebuds made from about 185g (6 oz) dark modelling chocolate, see page 32
6 ribbon loops and 4 tails, see page 34
5 chocolate leaves, see page 30
EQUIPMENT
bubblewrap
23cm (9 in) cake card

● Make the base on bubblewrap and place on the cake card.
● Make the background and stick to the base by dipping in chocolate and positioning.
● Join the two egg shells together and leave to set.
● To stick the egg to the base, spoon a small blob of chocolate on the base where the egg is to be stuck. When this starts to set, place the egg in position and it should stay. If you need to hold the egg in position for any length of time use cotton wool pads or gloves, not your fingers, as they can start to melt the chocolate and leave marks.
● If the join in the egg is not neat, it can be covered with a border, see page 48.
● Stick the roses, leaves and ribbon loops at the base of the egg with chocolate.

EXPERT ADVICE

≈

Thin cotton gloves, or the type made of thin plastic used by food handlers, are ideal for avoiding fingerprints on chocolate.

MAKING BORDERS FROM MODELLING CHOCOLATE

A quick and effective way of hiding or covering a join in a centrepiece or cake is to make a border from modelling chocolate. The rope is used in the birthday cake, see page 53, to cover the join between cake and board, and to edge a plaque, see page 51. Overlapping leaves are good way of hiding the join in an Easter egg.

~ 1 ~

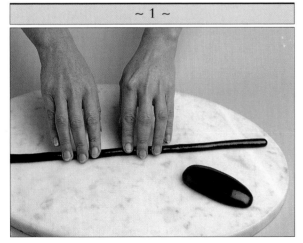

ROPE *Knead some modelling chocolate until smooth. Roll into a long sausage. Continue rolling lightly with your hand until a long, thin, even rope is formed.*

~ 2 ~

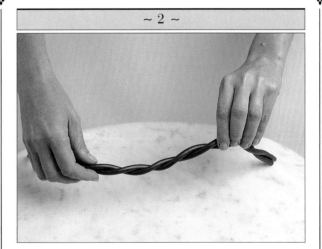

Make two of these and twist together to form a rope, or make three sausages and plait them.

~ 1 ~

LEAVES *Knead two colours of modelling paste gently together so they appear marbled and roll out thinly. Cut out with a leaf cutter. Press each leaf onto a veiner and leave to set before using.*

~ 2 ~

To form the border, stick the leaves in a line with a little chocolate, so they are overlapping and alternating left and right.

~ 1 ~

FLOWERS *Small chocolate flowers can be made from modelling chocolate to decorate eggs and plaques. Roll out a piece of modelling chocolate and cut out with a flower cutter. Cup the flowers and leave to harden on some bubblewrap until they hold their shape.*

~ 2 ~

Fill a piping bag with chocolate and pipe in the centres of the flowers. Leave to set and store for later use.

A MOTHER'S DAY PLAQUE

*M*others of all ages will adore this pretty plaque which they can display with pride before eating!

375g (12 oz) dark couverture
125g (4 oz) white couverture
375g (12 oz) dark modelling chocolate
125g (4 oz) white modelling chocolate
4 roses and 2 rosebuds, see page 32
7 large leaves, see page 30
assorted small flowers and leaves, see page 49
1 length chocolate rope, see page 48

EQUIPMENT
bubblewrap
greaseproof paper (parchment) piping bag

● Make a circular dark chocolate base on bubblewrap and at the same time make 7 large dark chocolate leaves. (For alternative base shapes, see below and page 70).

● With the modelling chocolate, make a selection of roses, leaves and flowers. On some, mix dark and white chocolate to achieve a mottled effect. Leave to harden.

● Make a length of chocolate rope and wrap it around the edge of the base.

● Arrange the roses and leaves on the side of the plaque and glue down with chocolate.

● Temper a little white chocolate and pipe on the message.

● Decorate the border with small leaves and flowers.

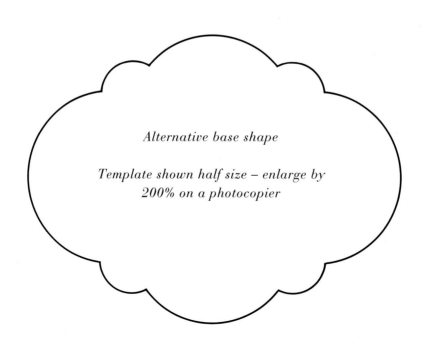

Alternative base shape

Template shown half size – enlarge by 200% on a photocopier

BUTTERFLY AND ROSES BIRTHDAY CAKE

*C*hocolate decorations are not just for adorning chocolate items. They also look stunning when used to provide a colour contrast on conventionally iced cakes. This example combines dark chocolate decorations with pretty pink icing.

20cm (8 in) round chocolate sponge cake
250g (8 oz) chocolate buttercream
750g (1½ lb) pale pink sugarpaste
250g (8 oz) dark modelling chocolate
1 length chocolate rope, see page 48
3 roses and 2 rosebuds, see page 32
6 dark chocolate leaves, see page 30
icing (confectioners') sugar, for dusting
1 butterfly runout, see page 54

● Cut the sponge cake in half and sandwich with buttercream. Cover the cake in a thin coat of buttercream to fill in any gaps and uneven patches and help the sugarpaste stick to the cake.

● Knead the sugarpaste until smooth, roll out and cover the cake. Smooth out any creases and leave for a few hours to firm up.

● Make a length of rope from modelling chocolate, wrap it around the base of the cake and cut to fit.

● Make a selection of chocolate roses and buds.

● Make 6 chocolate leaves. Lay them on a tray and gently dust with icing (confectioners') sugar.

● Arrange the roses and leaves on the cake and glue down with a little chocolate.

● To finish, stick a small runout butterfly opposite the flowers.

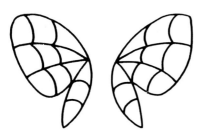

Butterfly template

EXPERT ADVICE

≈

The colour contrast could be reversed. Cover the cake with dark-coloured sugarpaste and decorate with pink modelling chocolate roses and milk chocolate leaves.

RUNOUTS

*R*unouts in chocolate are made using the same technique as royal icing runouts – an outline is piped first, with the centre flooded in. With chocolate, however, they are turned over when set to reveal the shiny underside, which always looks much neater. This technique is ideal for any decoration with an outline, such as a train on a children's cake. A butterfly design is ideal for decorating a chocolate cake or pudding, see page 53. Trace the butterfly wings from the template, see page 52, and lay on a flat board. Cover with a larger piece of acetate and secure with masking tape. Do not allow any pieces of acetate to stick out over the edge of the board as they may catch and break the runouts.

PIPING

*C*hocolate can be piped into a variety of shapes for decorative purposes or for writing names on Easter eggs and plaques. Chocolate couverture is normally thick enough to pipe lines and words, but for piping scrolls or stars with a piping tube (tip), the chocolate needs to be thickened slightly. This is achieved by tempering the couverture as usual and then adding glycerine or water drop-by-drop until the required consistency is reached. Do not add too much or it will become too thick to use. If this does happen, use it for fillings or in cooking.

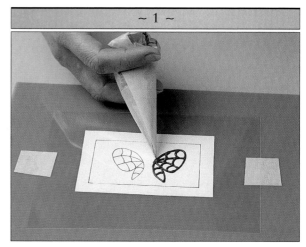

~ 1 ~

Temper some plain chocolate and spoon a small amount into a greaseproof paper (parchment) piping bag. Do not overfill . Cut off the end with scissors to leave a small hole similar in size to a no. 1 piping tube (tip). Pipe the outline of the butterfly and leave to set.

~ ❖ ~

***PIPED WORDS AND PATTERNS** Make a piping bag from greaseproof paper (parchment) and fill with chocolate (do not overfill). Cut a hole in the end similar to a no.1½ piping tube (tip). Use to pipe patterns and names. Complete in one go to avoid the chocolate setting in the bag.*

~ 2 ~

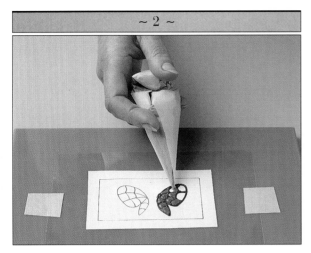

Temper some milk or white chocolate and fill a piping bag. Cut a hole in the end a little larger than for the outline and flood in the area inside. Do not worry about being too neat as the runouts are turned over (this is the underside). Leave to set.

~ 3 ~

Peel the wings off the acetate. Make a V-shaped template out of greaseproof paper and place the pair of wings upside-down in the centre of the V. Pipe a body in the centre using dark chocolate to join the wings together. When set, carefully remove and store away for later use.

~ ❖ ~

PIPEOUTS Trace a row of the chosen pattern (see page 71) onto paper and cover with greaseproof paper. Pipe over the shapes and leave to set slowly (if they cool too quickly they will curl up). When set, carefully peel off the greaseproof paper and store in a cool place.

~ ❖ ~

PIPED BORDERS USING PIPING TUBES (TIPS) Thicken chocolate to the consistency of royal icing (see page 17). Fit a greaseproof bag with a suitable piping tube (tip) and pipe out chocolate to form shells and scrolls. Work quickly to keep the chocolate flowing.

CUTOUTS

This technique is used on page 42 to make bases. Here, the same process is used to make small cutout shapes for decorating gâteaux, cakes and sweets. The only difference is whereas the large bases were cut with a hot cutter from a solid, hard sheet of chocolate, these small shapes are cut out when the chocolate sheet has just set but not hardened. This way, large numbers can be cut from a sheet very quickly. They are left to set hard and then peeled off the greaseproof paper (parchment).

~ ❖ ~

Spread a thin coat of chocolate onto greaseproof paper (parchment) and allow it to just set. Quickly spread over another thin coat and comb scrape a wavy pattern. When this is touch-dry, quickly cut out the shapes.

~ ❖ ~

Spread a coat of plain chocolate onto greaseproof paper (parchment) and leave until just touch-dry. Pipe white chocolate up and down to form the pattern. When touch-dry, cut out. They can be garnished with nuts to add some colour.

EXPERT ADVICE

≈

With cutouts, timing is important. If the chocolate is too soft the cutter will not cut a neat shape and the pattern can smear. If the chocolate is too hard, then the cutter will crack the sheet. Don't work in too cold a room. You will have longer to work with the chocolate before it sets hard.

CHOCOLATE CURLS AND SHAVINGS

*S*havings and curls are started in the same way – spread a thin layer of chocolate on a slab with a palette knife and leave until set but not too hard. The timing is important and it takes a little experience to get it just right.

CURLS To make petal-shaped curls, pull a round cutter towards you across the chocolate, paring off thin layers of chocolate petal shapes. Leave to set hard. These can be sprinkled randomly or arranged into a large flower on top of cakes and gâteaux. See page 63.

SHAVINGS To make shavings, push a metal scraper away from you over the chocolate to shave off thin slivers. Leave to set. Sprinkle on cakes and gâteaux for decoration.

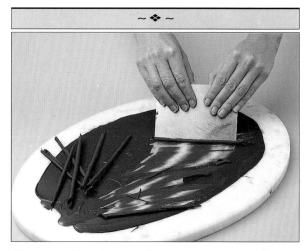

TUBES Chocolate tubes are very similar to shavings but instead of pushing the scraper straight, push diagonally across the chocolate to roll thin tubes. These are commonly used to garnish sweets, ice creams and gâteaux.

ENCASING A CAKE IN CHOCOLATE – 'EDGING'

To put that finishing touch to your chocolate gâteau or mousse, try this lovely edging which is both simple and inexpensive to make. Commercial borders can be bought in a variety of patterns, or you can make your own with a strip of acetate, see pages 60–61.

This elegant border is made by spinning white chocolate on the acetate before spreading with dark chocolate, see page 61. The top is decorated with rosettes of buttercream and chocolate pipeouts. Fill the centre with some dark chocolate sharings to finish.

The sides of a gâteau are just as important as the top, so do not limit yourself to a one-dimensional decoration. Introduce a colour contrast by using a touch of white chocolate or some luxurious gold flecks to compliment the richness of a dark chocolate gâteau.

~ 1 ~

Cut a strip of acetate to the same height as your sponge cake and trim the length so it fits exactly round the cake. Set aside. Cover the cake with cream, buttercream, or ganache and smooth with a scraper to create neat, even sides. Cool until the edge sets firmer.

~ 4 ~

Neatly wrap the strip around the cake until the ends join and leave to set. Wipe any smears of chocolate off the cake card.

~ 5 ~

Decorate the top of the cake. Piped rosettes of buttercream look superb decorated with pipeouts and shavings made from a mixture of white and milk chocolate.

~ 2 ~

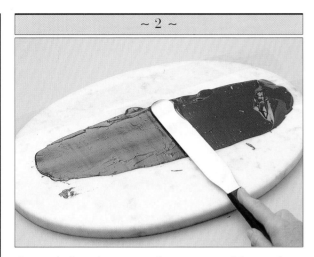

Spread chocolate over the acetate with a palette knife so a thin, even coat about 2.5mm (⅛ in) thick is achieved. Make sure there are no areas that are too thin as they will break when set.

~ 3 ~

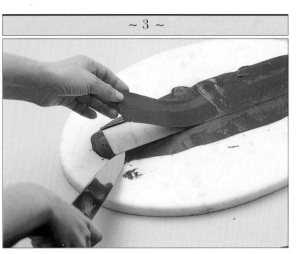

Find the edge of the acetate with a small knife and lift up. Clean the edges by running your finger down the edge of the strip.

~ 6 ~

When set and ready to serve, peel off the acetate to leave a shiny chocolate edging underneath.

The acetate strip could also be used on the inside of a flan ring or hoop to create a chocolate flan ring which can be filled with mousse and set in the refrigerator. When you have mastered the technique with a plain edge, try experimenting with different colours and patterns, see Variations, pages 62–65.

~ ❖ ~

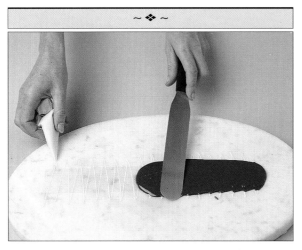

~ ❖ ~

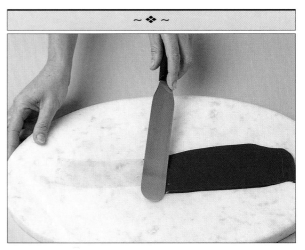

VARIATIONS Fill a piping bag with white chocolate and pipe a zigzag pattern overlapping the acetate strip. When touch-dry, spread on dark chocolate as usual.

On this commercial border, the pattern is already printed on the acetate with edible colour. Cut the required length of border and spread chocolate on as usual.

~ ❖ ~

~ ❖ ~

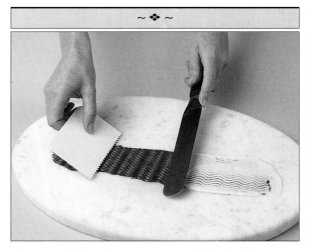

A marbled effect is created by dabbing on some blobs of dark chocolate then quickly pouring on some white chocolate. Using a pastry brush, swirl the chocolates around, pushing hard to create random patterns. Even out with a palette knife and continue as usual.

A striped border is more difficult but very effective. Spread dark chocolate as usual and firmly pull a comb scraper in a wavy line along the strip. When touch-dry, spread on white chocolate and continue as usual.

A commercial border with gold flecks and finished with dark chocolate is used to edge this gâteau. The top is decorated with dark chocolate curls, see page 58, pushed into the soft buttercream. Start at the centre and work outwards until the top is covered and resembles a large flower. Fill in any gaps with extra curls. The top can be lightly dusted with icing (confectioners') sugar if wished.

White chocolate can be used to provide stunning contrast. Make a marbled edge, see page 62. The top is decorated with two-tone shavings. Pour milk and white chocolate together on a marble slab and mix lightly before spreading.

Continue as usual. This finish is ideal for a white chocolate mousse or gâteau.

Here, a chocolate and hazelnut gâteau is decorated with a wavy patterned edge, made using a comb scraper, see page 62. Decorate the top with rosettes of buttercream, add a large striped bow to the centre and top with hazelnuts. To ring the changes, the hazelnuts could be replaced with glacé orange slices and the sponge could be flavoured with orange or covered in orange buttercream.

THE COUVERTURE IS TOO HEAVY AND THICK Influence of water or steam. If moisture in any form comes into contact with couverture it will cause it to thicken, rendering it useless for chocolate work. It can be used for cooking and fillings.

COUVERTURE LEFT TEMPERED TOO LONG BEFORE USING The fat has slowly solidified in the chocolate causing it to become puddingy. Reheat to 45°C (113°F) and repeat tempering process.

THE COUVERTURE HAS COOLED TOO MUCH Add some warm couverture or gently warm the bowl until the chocolate reaches the correct working temperature. This will not work if the chocolate has gone puddingy.

STREAKS APPEAR IN FINISHED PRODUCTS – 'FAT BLOOM' The working temperature is slightly too warm. Add some grated couverture and stir until it cools to the correct temperature.

STRIPES APPEAR ON THE FINISHED PRODUCTS The couverture is not properly mixed. The working temperature is too low. Stir thoroughly before and during use. Add warmer couverture to bring the temperature back to correct working temperature.

DURING STORAGE, THE CHOCOLATE DEVELOPS A DULL GREY BLOOM This is known as 'sugar bloom' and is caused by either damp storage conditions or changes in temperature causing condensation on the surface. The moisture melts the sugar in the chocolate which then crystallizes, causing a grey dusty effect on the surface. Make sure the storage area is at a constant cool temperature with no damp and good ventilation.

WHITE MARKS APPEAR ON DEMOULDED ITEMS The moulds were not dried properly. Water can become trapped in moulds with heavy patterns. Make sure they are completely dry before filling.

CRACKED ARTICLES If moulded items are placed in too cold a refrigerator, the chocolate contracts too fast and they will crack.

MOULDED ITEMS ARE DULL WHEN REMOVED FROM MOULD The moulds were greasy and not polished well, or items were left in the refrigerator too long.

These four chocolate golf bags show the various faults that can occur. Top left: the chocolate was not tempered correctly or too warm. The cocoa fat has separated from the mass and set in blotches and streaks – known as fat bloom. Top right: the mould was not polished properly, therefore the quality of the gloss has been lost. Bottom left: the chocolate piece has got damp in storage producing sugar bloom. Bottom right: there was water present in the mould because it was not dried properly.

*C*hocolate makes a lovely gift for any occasion. The addition of some glamorous gift wrapping adds that final touch to enhance the beauty of your creation, and keep it from the elements. The easiest and cheapest way to gift wrap chocolate is to use thin acetate wrapped around the piece, secured with a colourful bow.

● Acetate sheets can be bought plain or patterned, or special bags with card bases can be purchased from specialist suppliers. These are very good for Easter bunnies or other delicate figures that need to stand upright.

● Buying ready made bows can be expensive. It is both simple and inexpensive to make your own from the array of beautifully coloured ribbons available.

~ 1 ~

To make a bow, cut a length of florists' ribbon 90cm x 1.5cm (3 ft x ¾ in) and a narrow piece 30cm (12 in) long. Wrap the large ribbon round your fingers several times and press the ends to form a crease. Cut each corner off, leaving a thin piece in the centre.

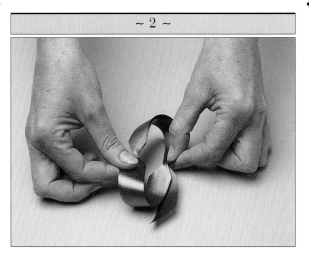

~ 2 ~

Push the two ends together until the thin pieces meet. Tie the thin strip of ribbon around the middle and secure with a double knot.

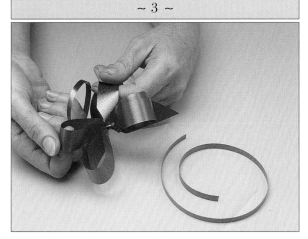

~ 3 ~

Hold each loop with your thumb and index finger and twist firmly to form the bow. Trim the ends of the tails with scissors.

TEMPLATES

Plaque shape variations
See page 50

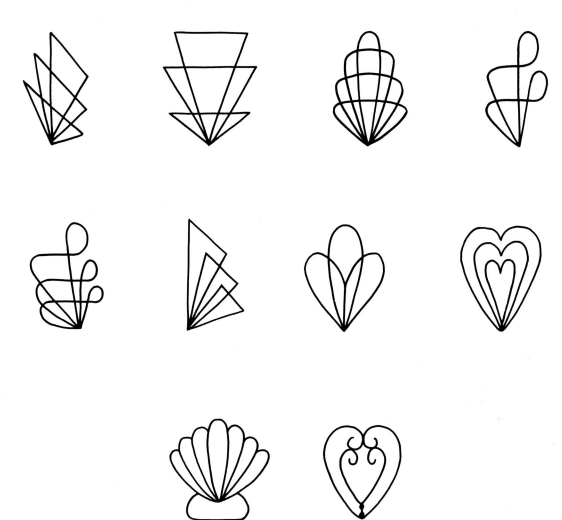

INDEX

FOR FURTHER INFORMATION

Merehurst is the leading publisher of cake decorating books and has an excellent range of titles to suit cake decorators of all levels. Please send for a free catalogue, stating the title of this book:

United Kingdom

Marketing Department
Merehurst Ltd.
Ferry House
51–57 Lacy Road
London SW15 1PR
Tel: 0181 780 1177
Fax: 0181 780 1714

U.S.A./Canada

Foxwood International Ltd.
Suite 426
420 Main Street East, Unit C
Milton, Ontario
L9T 5G3 Canada
Tel: 00 1 905 854 1305
Fax: 00 1 905 854 0978

Australia

J.B. Fairfax Ltd.
80 McLachlan Avenue
Rushcutters Bay
NSW 2011
Tel: (61) 2 361 6366
Fax: (61) 2 360 6262

Other Territories

For further information
contact:
International Sales
Department at United
Kingdom address.